GRIZZLY

GRIZZLY

Michio Hoshino

Chronicle Books • San Francisco

First published in the United States 1987 by
Chronicle Books, San Francisco
Copyright © 1986 by Michio Hoshino.
All rights reserved. No part of this book may be reproduced in
any form without written permission from the publisher.
Printed in Japan.
First published in Japan by Heibonsha, Publisher, Tokyo.
Library of Congress Cataloging-in-Publication Data
Hoshino, Michio, 1952 –
  Grizzly.
  Translation of: Gurizurī.
  1. Grizzly bear — Pictorial works.   I. Title.
QL737.C27H6713   1987   599.74'446
87-305
ISBN 0-87701-438-8
ISBN 0-87701-431-0 (pbk.)
Distributed in Canada by
Raincoast Books
112 East 3rd Avenue
Vancouver, B.C.
V5T 1C8
10 9 8 7 6 5 4

Chronicle Books
275 Fifth Street
San Francisco, California 94103

INTRODUCTION

I met Michio Hoshino about eight years ago when he first visited Alaska. He expressed a strong interest in Alaskan wildlife and in wildlife photography. As a Professor of Wildlife Management at the University of Alaska-Fairbanks, I see many young people who come to this state in love with the idea of studying animals and working in the wilderness of Alaska. Some also have an interest in a career in wildlife photography. Many of these young men and women lose heart as they become aware of the hard work required to get training as a modern naturalist or professional biologist. They also learn that not all fieldwork is done when the sun shines and the days are "picnic perfect." Michio has persisted in following his interests, learning a good deal about the biology and management of animals in Alaska, in both the field and the classroom, and developing skill as a wildlife photographer. He completed seven semesters of study at the University of Alaska-Fairbanks. During this time we talked many times. He was a student in one of my courses. I have been impressed by Michio's desire and determination.

Wildlife photography is a special and very demanding field. To do really good work one must not only master the purely photographic aspects, but it is essential as well that the photographer learn a great deal about the animals he or she will work with. In addition, those who do not have a true commitment to the work can never have the patience and persistence that is absolutely necessary. It is this understanding of the animals, a willingness to work in difficult weather and terrain, and the patience to wait for hours or even days to get one or two excellent shots that set the real wildlife photographer apart from the many roadside amateurs.

Michio has worked on this book for about six years, keeping the bears as a major effort while photographing other subjects as well. In the course of his travels, Michio has worked in many parts of Alaska that have not seen hordes of tourists; he seeks the wild country on its own terms. Many days while I was in Denali National Park conducting my own research on grizzly bears, I have watched Michio observing these interesting animals, getting to know them through hours of watching, and then "reaching out" with his telephoto lenses to record intimate moments in the relationship of mother and young as well as dramatic action in the life of bears. Michio has gained my respect as an individual who is rapidly developing his ability as a wildlife photographer. He has clearly put together a series of photographs that combine a great deal of beauty and experience with the life of the grizzly bears in Alaska. I hope that the harsh weather and the long waits do not discourage him for many years to come. He has become a cheerful friend and regularly has some excellent photographs to show me that clearly emphasize the value of his apprenticeship in the Alaskan wilderness.

Frederick C. Dean
Professor of Wildlife-Management
University of Alaska-Fairbanks

FOREWORD

After eight years of perilous duty picking our way through the political minefields surrounding any governor's office, my wife Bella and I vastly enjoy life on our remote wilderness homestead some 150 miles from the nearest traffic light or hamburger stand. It is only with immense provocation and great reluctance that we venture out of the hills into the hazards of "civilization." Similarly, we do not enthusiastically encourage civilization's encroachment upon our domain.

Since the only way to reach our location is by small aircraft, sometimes months will go by without visitors. Other than relatives or close friends, those who do come usually are on some sort of professional assignment: archeologists, biologists, game wardens, or members of the media. Like most politicians I have grown a bit gun shy of the last. Hence the presence of unknown media people can create some suspicious tension. Thus we were not exactly exuberant when asked if a photographer could spend a few days with us taking pictures for an article for which I had agreed to be interviewed.

My introduction to Michio Hoshino was made in the teeth of a howling winter wind as I drove my tractor to meet him on the beach where the small aircraft had dropped him off.

He quickly established himself as an extremely competent professional, exceptionally considerate house guest, and wizard on a wood stove. He won Bella's heart by taking over the cooking chores and conjuring up delicious meals from exotic ingredients he had brought with him. He won our respect as an extraordinarily accomplished photographer with samplings of his work gleaned from major Japanese and U.S. publications such as *Smithsonian*.

I had pretty much hung up my guns years ago, but after almost forty years in Alaska as a professional hunter and guide I have some appreciation for the dedication, woodcraft, endurance, and innovation required for a successful hunt. Michio has all these qualities in abundance. He is indeed a mighty hunter. However, in these days when I have found that far too often the hunted out-nobles the hunter, I especially appreciate that Michio's lust is for life instead of blood. His superb photographic trophies bring a vibrant touch of immortality and splendor to Alaska's wild creatures far more rewarding and impressive than some grizzled decapitation grinning down from a den wall.

Michio, old friend, come back anytime at all—just don't forget the soy sauce.

Jay Hammond
Former Governor
of Alaska

Previous page: A strong wind stirs the austere winter landscape of the Alaska Range. Somewhere soon in this world of fifty degrees below zero, a now hibernating grizzly will give birth.

Above: The winters of the far north are long and dark. Curtains of the aurora borealis, undulating like a living creature, cascade over the endless taiga.

The Big Dipper seen through the aurora. The Big Dipper is the
motif on the Alaska state flag.

SPRING

Thirteen years have passed since my first encounter with a grizzly. At that time I was living with an Alaskan Eskimo family in a village called Shishmaref on the Arctic Circle. My long-time dream of visiting Alaska had been realized.

One day we set off by boat for a one-week caribou hunting trip. Descending one of the nameless rivers, which flow through the Arctic Circle like the mesh of a vast net, we searched for caribou herds. Spruce closed in on the eroded river banks. Mother and calf moose appeared along the beaches. The scenes that appeared before my eyes as we traveled down the river seemed to come right out of Seaton's world — a world about which I had read with great fascination as a child. These scenes were particularly reminiscent of a travelogue from his later years, *Searching for Wildlife on the Arctic Prairies*. That night, pitching the tent on the river bank and sitting around the campfire with an Eskimo family, I realized that I had arrived in that incredibly distant world.

The next day, climbing a mountain that commanded a fine view, we searched for caribou herds. My eyes focused on a brownish gray lump, leisurely moving through the vast expanse of undulating tundra. It was my first grizzly. The harsh arctic wilderness is not a place in which you find wildlife wherever you go. The grizzly was the only creature that moved through this almost dizzingly vast open space. I felt an intense awareness of existence itself. It was as if I had seen an animal in the wild for the first time.

Even after we killed some caribou and returned to the Eskimo village, the events of that day lingered in my heart. In particular, the image of the grizzly wandering through the Alaskan wilderness was indelibly blazed in my mind.

Following pages: The long winter is over and grizzly cubs, born deep in a den during midwinter, experience sunlight for the first time. Bathed in the warm light of spring, a sow and cubs walk through the Alaska Range.

The highest mountain in North America, Mount McKinley is
still covered by a veil of snow. However, the snow has begun to
melt on the surrounding mountains.

Pages 14–21: Many birds and mammals of the far north, including the grizzly are predators of the arctic ground squirrel. Although a grizzly will invade the nest of a ground squirrel, its success rate is low. And when one considers the energy necessary to dig up such a nest and the size of the prey in question, it does not seem like a very profitable undertaking. Sometimes a ground squirrel will come up through one of its passageways and watch from behind as a grizzly frantically digs

up its nest. Although a grizzly's main diet is plant material, this is probably not out of choice but necessity. If meat is available, even in the form of so small a creature as a ground squirrel, this becomes the preferred food source.

Salmon swim upstream to spawn, where a hungry grizzly waits.

SUMMER

My first experiences in Alaska at age nineteen left a very deep impression. Even after returning to Japan, I constantly felt the summons of the Alaskan wilderness. I resolved that my next experience in Alaska would not be a short trip—I wanted to live there.

Six years later my life in Alaska began, and I embarked upon a career of capturing the wilderness through photography. I lived for half a year at a time in a tent, leisurely walking through and studying the natural environment around me. Although overwhelmed by the colossal scope of the arctic wilderness, I found that little by little Alaska was opening her doors for me. And, before I knew it, seven years had gone by.

Alaska is a world of phenomenal scale, of primitiveness and purity. There are few species of life, and the food chains are relatively simple. In other words, it is a world in which the arctic ecosystem is held in a delicate balance. Nature here may be the most vulnerable to change, the most easily scarred, of all places in the world. Even the grizzly, standing at the peak of the food chain, cannot escape this destiny.

Walking through the Alaskan mountains I came upon grizzlies time and time again. One spring day I spotted a grizzly sow and cub playing in the lingering snow. They were in the midst of a game of tag. When the cub ran away, the sow would pursue it. These actions were repeated many times, until the sow finally caught the cub. I burst out laughing at the scene that followed, as the mother bear continued to play with her young. The sow firmly grasped the cub with two paws and rolled down the mountain slope, the cub in her arms. As I watched this heartwarming scene, I could not help reflecting upon the tragic path that characterizes the history of the grizzly.

The history of the settling of America is at the same time the history of the massacre of the grizzly. Labeled as a fierce animal, the grizzly continues to be slaughtered. Alaska provides the only sizable habitat remaining to this bear.

Previous pages: The season of new green arrives. The days
lengthen and tundra life undergoes rapid growth. Lovely
arctic flowers lift their faces. A new life begins for the
grizzly cubs.

Above and following: In the spring forest a sow plays with her cub. Observing the infinite gentleness in the sow's eyes as she gazed at her cub, all my own tension vanished.

27

Right: The grizzly possesses a fairly well defined territory and will move about within its boundaries as the seasons change.

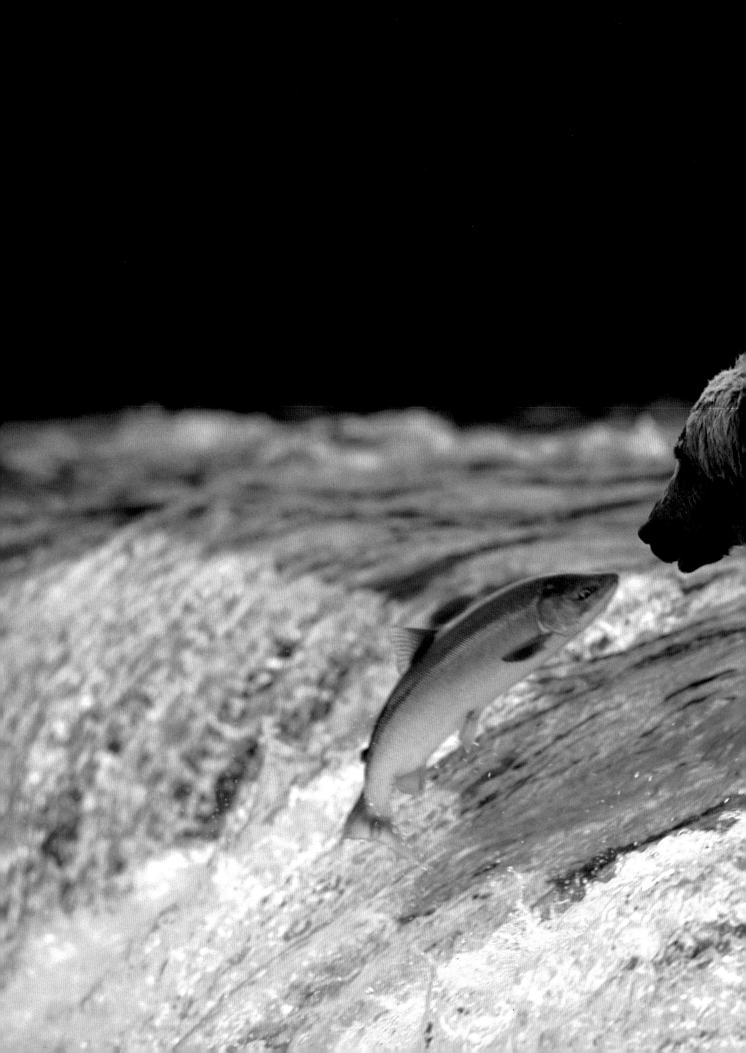

Pages 30–35: Summer comes to Alaska and salmon devote
all their energy to swimming upstream to spawn, even
ascending waterfalls. Grizzlies skillfully use their mouths
and the sharp claws on their front paws to catch salmon
weighing several pounds. The drama of the brief arctic summer,
featuring the grizzly and the salmon, has begun.

Previous pages: Many grizzlies gather in search of salmon.
Because bears are very territorial animals, the stronger ones will
occupy places where the salmon are easiest to catch and will not
allow other bears to approach.

Above: Grizzlies are shrewd and fast. They can run for great distances and even through water without decreasing their speed.

Pages 40–43: When the salmon are at their peak, the grizzlies will eat only the most nourishing portions of the fish, the head and the eggs. I witnessed many scenes in which a bear would pin down a salmon with its paw, look it over, and then release it uneaten. Bears may be able to distinguish male and female salmon.

Following pages: Fights over salmon fishing grounds can usually be avoided by recognizing relative strengths. However, when bears of equal strength run into each other, they will fight to establish territorial rights.

Left: From spring to summer, nursing periods grow gradually longer. In a summer meadow a sow patiently suckles her young.

Above: This is the cubs' first summer, and the world around them is full of unknowns.

Following pages: Shafts of evening light shine through gaps between clouds, illuminating the tundra. The grizzly and her cubs are a part of this vast landscape of the far north.

Left and above: I came across a wolf in a meadow. I had been observing it for a while, when suddenly a grizzly appeared from behind the wolf, pursuing it at great speed. As they drew closer together, they disappeared from sight into a valley. Ordinarily the grizzly and wolf will occupy the same territory, ignoring the presence of the other. However, if a grizzly happens to find prey downed by the wolf, the wolf will, in most cases, relinquish it to the bear.

The first snows on the mountains and the turning of the leaves
at their base occur at the same time. One can smell winter in the
air.

AUTUMN TO WINTER

One autumn I set up basecamp in the middle of grizzly habitat. As I was sitting before my campfire one night, a sow and cubs appeared out of the forest just in front of me. The two cubs stood up on their hind feet, and after observing me for some time with their mother, vanished back into the forest. At this time of year the grizzly puts on large quantities of fat for the winter by eating blueberries and soapberries, or wandering down to the river to eat the salmon, which have finished spawning.

Almost every night I heard the distant howl of wolves. It seemed as though one pack had separated into several groups. Apparently the howling served to ascertain the location of each group. Each group would begin, as if making overtures to the rest, and in the end they would howl in a fixed chorus. The howling left behind a penetrating swell, which echoed throughout the early winter mountains. I was overcome with joy at this realization of the storybook world I had read about as a child. Although I was all alone, without any weapons, I had not the slightest fear. Thus I sensed in the howling of the wolves a mysterious harmony, as their voices reached an accord with the forces of nature around them.

At the end of my trip it began to snow. The first aurora borealis of the season danced in the northern sky, telling of the coming of winter. When I was coming down out of the mountains, I ran into a grizzly sow and cub frolicking in the new snow. The cub, born during the winter in the sow's den, had grown a great deal. It was running about, covered with snow. But, it would be one more winter before it parted from its mother. In about one more month it would be beginning its long winter sleep.

Following pages: The brief autumn has arrived. At the end of August, the tundra is reborn as a crimson carpet. As new snow falls on mountain peaks, a symphony of color marks the turning of the seasons.

Above and right: At this time of year the tundra is replete with ripened berries — blueberries, cranberries, soapberries, and others — which become the chief component of the bears' diet.

Following pages: Siblings, after leaving their mother during their
third year, will often stay together for a time.

Above: A grizzly, immersed in a sea of golden grass.

Following pages: A silhouetted grizzly cuts through a lakeside forest.

Above: As the sun sets on an evening of the short autumn season, a grizzly searches for salmon in a lake.

Following pages: A grizzly shakes off the frigid waters of early winter.

Left: Preparing for winter, the grizzly puts on weight by eating its fill of salmon.

Above: Cubs born during winter denning, have already grown this much.

Following pages: Winter approaches. The days grow shorter and the sunlight gets thinner each day.

Above and right: Cubs play under falling white flakes — their first snowfall.

Following pages: By this time, salmon, weakened from spawning, are easily caught.

Above: Winter draws near and the grizzly must return to the
mountains.

Following pages: This grizzly must prepare the den in which she and her cubs will spend the next six months. Have they put on enough weight to tide them through the winter?